We Can Trust the Bible

STUDENT GUIDE

> Forever, O LORD, Your word is settled in heaven. Your faithfulness endures to all generations; You established the earth, and it abides.—Psalm 119:89–90

GOD'S WORD FOR ALL GENERATIONS

D1273360

Answers
BIBLE CURRICULUM

Answers Bible Curriculum

Year 1 • Quarter 1 • Junior High Student

Printed in China

Contents

Introduction to Answers Bible Curriculum. 5

1 God's Word Is Our Foundation 7
    Prepare to Learn 8
    Studying God's Word 11
    Psalm 19 Study Sheet 11
    God's Word in the Real World. 12
    Prayer Requests. 14

2 Studying the Bible 15
    Prepare to Learn 16
    Studying God's Word 19
    Bible Study Guidelines Bookmarks 20
    God's Word in the Real World. 20
    Prayer Requests. 22

3 God's Word Guides Us. 23
    Prepare to Learn 24
    Studying God's Word 27
    Impossible for God?. 27
    God's Word in the Real World. 27
    Prayer Requests. 28

4 God Preserves His Word. 29
    Prepare to Learn 30
    Studying God's Word 33
    God's Word in the Real World. 34
    Prayer Requests. 34

5 God's Word Is Complete. 35
    Prepare to Learn 36
    Studying God's Word 39
    A Common Thread 39
    God's Word in the Real World. 40
    Prayer Requests. 40

6 Don't Change God's Word 41
    Prepare to Learn 42
    Studying God's Word 46
    A Different Gospel 47
    God's Word in the Real World. 47
    Prayer Requests. 48

7 Starting with Scripture..**49**

    Prepare to Learn 50

    Studying God's Word 53

    Foolproof Apologetics Video Notes 53

    God's Word in the Real World....................................... 54

    Prayer Requests.. 56

8 How Do I Know God Exists?...**57**

    Prepare to Learn 58

    Studying God's Word 61

    God's Word in the Real World....................................... 62

    Prayer Requests.. 62

9 What Is God Like?..**63**

    Prepare to Learn 64

    Studying God's Word 67

    God's Word in the Real World....................................... 68

    Prayer Requests.. 68

10 The Trinity..**69**

    Prepare to Learn 70

    Studying God's Word 73

    Trinitarian Heresies 74

    God's Word in the Real World....................................... 74

    Prayer Requests.. 74

11 The Seven C's of History...**75**

    Prepare to Learn 76

    Studying God's Word 80

    Comparing the Views... 80

    God's Word in the Real World....................................... 80

    Prayer Requests.. 80

12 What Is the Gospel?...**81**

    Prepare to Learn 82

    Studying God's Word 86

    The Gospel Through the Seven C's of History 86

    God's Word in the Real World....................................... 86

    Prayer Requests.. 88

13 Value of a Biblical Worldview..**89**

    Prepare to Learn 90

    Studying God's Word 92

    God's Word in the Real World....................................... 93

    Prayer Requests.. 94

Introduction to Answers Bible Curriculum

We hear many competing truth-claims in our culture today. Scientists claim to be able to "prove" many things, including what happened in the distant past. There are a multitude of religions and faiths, all claiming to have the one "truth." Even within the church we are bombarded by conflicting Christian TV programs, books, etc., each teaching with authority on topics ranging from marriage to prophecy to counseling to evangelism to heaven and hell. What are we to make of it? And how can we possibly sort out truth from error, or even the good from the bad?

You are starting a journey of discovery into God's Word, the Bible. Over the next 13 weeks we will be looking at what the Bible is, where it came from, who wrote it, why we can trust it, and how God intends to use it in our lives. Beyond that, we'll begin to explore who this God is who revealed His mind and will through the pages of Scripture. What is He like? What are His attributes? How might our view of God be distorted?

We think you'll find this program different from any you have taken before. You will not only learn what's in the Bible, but you'll learn why it's there, why it's true, and how to defend it. Your questions will be answered, your faith encouraged, and your view of God expanded.

We encourage you to read the Prepare to Learn section before class each week. This will provide important background information so that you will get more from the lesson.

For more information and links to online articles and videos, be sure to visit the Online Resource Page at www.AnswersBibleCurriculum.com.

God's Word Is Our Foundation

1

Key Passages

- Psalm 19:7–11, 86:11, 119:105

What You Will Learn

- How to use the Bible as the starting point for making decisions.
- The qualities of God's Word.
- What the ultimate source of problems is in our society.

Lesson Overview

As God's Word, the Bible must be the foundation for all areas in our lives. It is important for us to understand our worldview and ensure it is founded in Scripture.

Memory Verse

Psalm 19:7–9
The law of the Lord is perfect, converting the soul;
the testimony of the Lord is sure, making wise the simple;
the statutes of the Lord are right, rejoicing the heart;
the commandment of the Lord is pure, enlightening the eyes;
the fear of the Lord is clean, enduring forever;
the judgments of the Lord are true and righteous altogether.

📖 Prepare to Learn

SCRIPTURAL BACKGROUND

Ever since Satan in the form of a serpent cast doubt on God's instructions in the Garden of Eden (Genesis 3:1–4), people have questioned the authority of God's Word. As descendants of Adam, we have inherited a sinful nature (Romans 5:12, Romans 3:23; 1 John 1:8–10), which corrupts our human reasoning, questions God's authority, and prevents us from embracing the truth.

The Bible says, "Your word is a lamp to my feet and a light to my path" (Psalm 119:105). This reminds us that we cannot move along the path of life without God's Word providing the light of truth to guide us. The Bible enables us to see the world as it truly is. Without the understanding that Scripture gives, we are lost in the dark, wondering how to accurately interpret good and evil, God and man, right and wrong. We are left with a distorted view of history, science, and society. The testimony of the Lord, however, is undistorted and sure (Psalm 19:7).

In Psalm 19, King David powerfully reveals the supremacy of Scripture. The perfection of the Word leads to conversion of the soul, the surety of the Word brings wisdom, the righteousness of the Word rejoices the heart, and the purity of the Word lights the way. The Word of God is clean, true, and righteous, producing the fear of the Lord necessary for repentance. Verse 11 summarizes the intention of the Word—that we may be warned to keep the commandments and achieve the promised reward.

Those who stand in awe of God, who are bound to Him without compromise, and who submit their minds to the teaching of Scripture are those who have a solid foundation and are able to connect the Bible to real life.

Our response to God and His Word should be to join the psalmist in praying, "Teach me Your way, O Lord; I will walk in Your truth; unite my heart to fear Your name" (Psalm 86:11).

APOLOGETICS BACKGROUND

The proper role of apologetics is to confirm what we know of God through His Word. It is not a series of explanations attempting to prove that the Bible is true or that there is a God.

As Christians, we start with the assumption that God exists and that His Word is true. This serves as the starting point for our beliefs. This is called presuppositional thinking because we are presupposing that what God says about Himself is true.

Jesus set the example for us in this way of thinking through His life, ministry, and teaching. All of

Jesus's messages presupposed that the Scriptures were true.

He knew the Scriptures so well that learned men marveled (John 7:15).

He quoted Scripture as historical fact, referencing some of the most-attacked accounts in the Bible, including Creation (Matthew 19:4–5), Noah and the Flood (Matthew 24:37–39), Sodom and Gomorrah (Matthew 10:15, 11:23–24), Lot and his wife (Luke 17:28–32), and Jonah and the fish (Matthew 12:39–41).

He said the writings of Moses are more powerful than even someone rising from the dead (Luke 16:29–31).

He defended Himself against Satan with God's Word (Matthew 4:4–10).

In the same way, we must rely on God's Word as the starting point for all of our judgments and beliefs. Others may insist that we "leave the Bible out of it" when discussing God, creation, absolute truth, morality, science, or the Bible itself. However, we cannot and must not. Christians stand on the Word of God—it is our foundation (Luke 6:47–49). Everything we believe and how we live are based on what it says.

Disregarding the Scriptures would result in disaster because our foundation would be destroyed. Our starting point is and must always be the Bible. If we give up our starting point—our foundation—we will lose the battle before it begins. We must assume that the Bible is the trustworthy starting point from which we interpret all of life.

HISTORICAL BACKGROUND

We are no longer a culture that depends on God's Word. Today people doubt that the Bible's history is even true. The history of mankind shows over and over that when the Bible is rejected, then man himself becomes the measure of all things. How have we gotten to this age of man-centeredness?

Ever since the Garden of Eden, there has been a battle over the authority of the Word of God. The serpent asked Eve, "Did God really say that?" (See Genesis 3:1.) And the Apostle Paul warns us that just as the serpent deceived Eve so our minds can be corrupted to believe lies that deny biblical truth (2 Corinthians 11:3).

The book of Genesis provides the foundation for the Bible and the gospel message of redemption. It wasn't too long ago that Genesis was taken literally and there was little controversy over its interpretation.

In the late 1700s and early 1800s, the history of Genesis came under attack by scientists who began to accept the idea of millions of years of history rather than the thousands of years God records in His Word.

This interpretation brought compromise in the areas of biology—Darwinian evolution replacing God's creation of kinds; geology—millions of years replacing the Flood history of Genesis; anthropology—man descended from ape-like ancestors replacing God's creation of man in His own image; astronomy—the big bang replacing God's amazing account of speaking the universe into existence.

As our culture has adopted these secular views, the Bible has been disconnected from reality and consequently is becoming less and less relevant. Even many in the church have separated "church" life from "all other" life. These compromises have torn down the foundations of biblical authority and trust in God's Word. The result? Jesus gave us the answer when He asked Nicodemus, "If I have told you earthly things and you do not believe, how will you believe if I tell you heavenly things?" (John 3:12).

Many no longer believe the earthly things that Jesus was referring to. And, consequently, even the heavenly things—redemption, hope, eternity with God, forgiveness, Christ's Resurrection, the Trinity, and judgment—are no longer of any interest to us. It is time to get back to the foundational teachings of the Word of God, beginning in Genesis.

For more information on this topic, see the Online Resource Page.

 Studying God's Word

What are the biggest problems in our society today?

- Contrevery with the Bible
- People don't know what they believe

Take notes as you study the following passages.

Psalm 86:11

Teach me about the bible

Psalm 119:105

 Psalm 19 Study Sheet

Complete the Psalm 19 study sheet.

God's Word in the Real World

1. Everyone with whom you interact has a worldview. In what areas do you see someone's worldview having the most impact on an individual's life?

   - At school
   - At their place of worship
   - In a conversation

2. Where do you see a difference in worldview causing conflict in your life?

   - ~~At my house~~
   - My mom doesn't

3. Why do people reject the Bible as the absolute authority?

   - Because of what other men have said throughout history
   - Satan
   - Because Adam/Eve ate the apple.

4. How might you attempt to change a person's understanding of the Bible's authority and reliability?

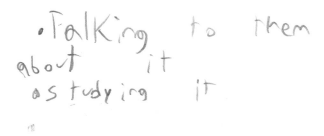

Talking to them about it
studying it

5. After thinking about the authority of the Bible in light of the problems we noted in society, has your view of the true problem changed? How?

Nope

 **Prayer Requests**

- Book fair
- Koronavirus
- Heal sick
- Forgive sin

2

Studying the Bible

Key Passages

- Hebrews 4:11–13; 2 Timothy 2:14–19, 3:16

What You Will Learn

- The three parts of the inductive Bible study method.

- How to distinguish between exegesis and eisegesis.

- Why it is important to carefully study the Bible.

Lesson Overview

The inductive Bible study method is a tool that allows us to understand what Scripture is teaching and how to apply it to our lives. Drawing ideas out of the text by asking good questions and understanding context will help us avoid twisting God's Word to suit our own desires.

Memory Verse

Psalm 19:7–9
The law of the Lord is perfect, converting the soul;
the testimony of the Lord is sure, making wise the simple;
the statutes of the Lord are right, rejoicing the heart;
the commandment of the Lord is pure, enlightening the eyes;
the fear of the Lord is clean, enduring forever;
the judgments of the Lord are true and righteous altogether.

Prepare to Learn

SCRIPTURAL BACKGROUND

God has revealed Himself to us in the words of the Bible—His only written revelation to man. We are called to study diligently what has been revealed and to apply it to the way we live our lives. Within the pages of Scripture, we find many exhortations to use what God has revealed in a way that honors Him.

In the Old Testament, we find examples of the Israelites abandoning what God had revealed to them. As a result, the people of that nation became corrupt.

We see in Nehemiah 8 the reading of the book of the Law of Moses before the assembly of Israel after it had been neglected for so long. Hearing the words, the people again understood what God required of them and sought to live accordingly.

Jesus chided the scribes and Pharisees for their failure to understand what God had revealed. "Have you not read?" was His way of pointing out their misunderstandings (see Matthew 12:3–5, 19:4, 22:31). They had added their own ideas into the Scriptures rather than seeking to understand the plain meaning.

As Jesus taught, He constantly referenced the Scriptures as authoritative for guiding our lives. That same idea persisted as the apostles and disciples continued to spread the gospel after Christ's ascension.

In Acts 17:10–12, we read of the Bereans, who were commended for searching the Scriptures to confirm what Paul was teaching.

In the New Testament epistles, there are many examples of examining the Bible to understand the truth. For example, in Hebrews 4:11–13 we are told that the Bible is like a sword that helps us discern truth from error in our thoughts. And Paul exhorted Timothy to study diligently God's Word in order to discern what is true (2 Timothy 2:14–19).

We trust that God has revealed to us those things that we need to live lives that honor Him. Peter relates this idea to us in 2 Peter 1:2–4 when he tells us that "all things that pertain to life and godliness" have been given to us "through the knowledge of Him." How do we know about God? We know primarily by what He has revealed to us in His Word. The doctrine known as the *sufficiency of Scripture* doesn't mean that the Bible is an exhaustive manual on everything, but that its principles are sufficient to guide us in the different situations we face.

In this lesson, we will teach the three-step inductive study method which will then be used throughout this curriculum to discern what the text of Scripture says. Laying such a foundation is critical if we are to study the Bible in a way that will not distort the text or make it conform to our thoughts. We are to submit ourselves to the Scriptures, not the other way around.

APOLOGETICS BACKGROUND

Many people chide Christians for reading the Bible literally. The Bible contains many different types of literature, but all of them communicate God's truth to us. When we say we take the Bible literally, we really mean that we take it in the sense that it was written. Some sections of Scripture are meant to be read as historical accounts, while others are poetic.

The process of understanding what Scripture says is called *hermeneutics*—a big word describing the process of trying to understand what the Bible means. Learning proper hermeneutics opens a whole new world of truth found in the Bible. There are many different schools of biblical interpretation. These range from liberal approaches (mystical interpretation, naturalistic interpretation, etc.) to the more conservative approach we'll be using (where ideas are considered in context and Scripture is used to interpret Scripture). This second, more conservative method may be new to you. It is often referred to as the grammatical-historical method of interpretation because it takes into account the grammar and context of the passage as well as the historical and cultural setting of the author and the original hearers.

As Christians, we recognize that the Bible is God's very breath revealing His words to us. As we seek to understand what He has said, we should not import our own ideas into Scripture but rather allow Scripture to inform and evaluate our ideas. Drawing ideas out of the text is called *exegesis* (ex- meaning "out of"), while adding our ideas into the text is called *eisegesis* (eis- meaning "into").

Take Genesis 1 for example. If we simply read that chapter as it is plainly written, we would conclude that God created the universe in six normal days—an accurate exegesis. On the other hand, if we consider that same text by starting with a belief in evolutionary processes occurring over millions of years, we might be tempted instead to interpret those "days" as long ages. In that case, we would engage in eisegesis since we imported the idea of long ages into the text—a practice that can lead to the dangers of compromise and distorted conclusions.

In order to properly exegete a passage, we include three essential components in an inductive Bible study: observation, interpretation, and application. These steps can be subdivided in various ways, but we will stick to three basic parts to teach the process.

To **observe**, we simply ask *who*, *what*, *where*, *when*, *why*, and *how* questions about the study passage. Who is the author writing to? What words are repeated or emphasized in the passage? Where is the event taking place? When was this written? What type of literature is being used (history, poetry, parable, etc.)? What is the main point of the passage?

By taking time to observe the text, we become familiar with the important words, commands, and main themes that are present. Once we are familiar with the passage, we are ready to interpret what we have read.

To **interpret**, we look at the passage in light of what the rest of the Bible has to say on the same topic. We may identify cross-references, cultural considerations, specific word meanings, context, commentaries, or parallel passages that tell of the same account or provide the same idea. We should be careful during the interpretation stage because there is always the danger of trying to read our own ideas into the text.

After we have observed what the text says and interpreted the key ideas, the next step is to **apply** the Word to daily life. Scripture is full of God's commands to believers to apply what He has communicated—we are to be doers of the Word, not just hearers (James 1:21–24).

Scripture is profitable to us when we apply its teaching to one or more of the four areas identified in 2 Timothy 3:16–17:

- *Doctrine* (understanding of fundamental truths)
- *Reproof* (pointing out sin)
- *Correction* (identifying right actions)
- *Instruction in righteousness* (living by God's commands and principles)

The Word may expose an error in their thinking or a flaw in the way they are living and thus present an opportunity to repent of those sins and to be conformed to the image of Christ.

In summary, right theology leads to right living. We can praise God for the grace He has shown us by saving us and sanctifying us. We can ask Him to mature us and change us into the image of His Son through the power of His Spirit.

HISTORICAL BACKGROUND

Evangelical tradition is built on the understanding that every Christian can read and understand God's Word. The fancy term for this idea is the *perspicuity of Scripture*. The reformers fought to make the Bible available in the language of the people—a privilege we enjoy today—in stark contrast with the teaching of other groups who historically opposed the idea.

The fear that motivated this opposition was that people would take the Bible and misunderstand and misapply it. This has indeed happened on occasion, but those who distort the Scriptures do so "to their own destruction" (2 Peter 3:14–18). Many cults and false religions have been founded on careless use or intentional distortion of the Bible. This makes it all the more important that we handle God's Word carefully.

For more information on this topic, see the Online Resource Page.

Studying God's Word

What do you know about hermeneutics?

Take notes as you study the following passages.

Hebrews 4:11–13

2 Timothy 2:14–19

2 Timothy 3:16

Bible Study Guidelines Bookmarks

Complete the Bible Study Guidelines bookmark.

God's Word in the Real World

1. How will this lesson impact the way you study the Bible?

2. How would you explain the difference between exegesis and eisegesis in your own words or in an analogy?

3. What are the positive and negative aspects of having access to several different Bible translations?

4. Whose responsibility is it to make sure you understand the Bible?

5. Which step of the inductive study method offers the most opportunity to twist the Scripture or add personal ideas into the text? How can you guard against that?

6. What Bible study tools do you have access to that might help you in this process?

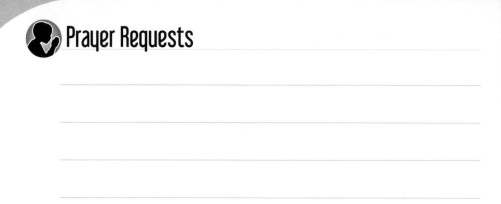
Prayer Requests

God's Word Guides Us

3

Key Passages

- 2 Timothy 3:16–17; 2 Peter 1:19–21; Titus 1:2; Hebrews 6:13–18

What You Will Learn

- To recognize that God's Word is true because He cannot lie.

- The roles of God and men in writing the Bible.

- The four ways God's Word guides us according to Scripture.

Lesson Overview

All Scripture is inspired by God, who cannot lie. It is useful for teaching, reproof, correction, and instruction in righteousness.

Memory Verse

Psalm 19:7–9
The law of the Lord is perfect, converting the soul;
the testimony of the Lord is sure, making wise the simple;
the statutes of the Lord are right, rejoicing the heart;
the commandment of the Lord is pure, enlightening the eyes;
the fear of the Lord is clean, enduring forever;
the judgments of the Lord are true and righteous altogether.

📖 Prepare to Learn

SCRIPTURAL BACKGROUND

In his second letter to Timothy, Paul stated, "All Scripture is given by inspiration of God" (2 Timothy 3:16–17). The Bible is the inspired ("breathed out") Word of God, transmitted not by the will of man, but through holy men of God as they were directed by the Holy Spirit (2 Peter 1:20–21). These men, under the inspiration of the Holy Spirit, wrote all that God instructed without error. It is the only inerrant, infallible Word of God, and we can trust it to guide us in all things.

How does it guide us? Paul tells us that it is useful for doctrine—teaching Christian truth; reproof—telling us when we are wrong; correction—showing us how to correct our wrong actions; and instruction in righteousness—teaching us how to obey God (2 Timothy 3:16–17). These are the general guidelines—they are expounded on again and again throughout the Bible.

God has spoken to reveal His plan for history, His purpose for mankind, and His will for us. More than 2,000 times the Old Testament states, "Thus says the Lord," or something similar, claiming that God Himself is the author. In the New Testament we observe that Jesus preached the Word of God (Luke 5:1), the early church preached the Word of God (Acts 4:31), the Word of God was preached to the Gentiles (Acts 11:1), and Paul preached the Word of God throughout all of his missionary journeys (Acts 13:5, 18:11, 19:10).

The Word of God is living and active (Hebrews 4:12), given to us by God Himself—to teach us the principles of our faith, to reveal our sin, to show us how to deal with sin, to instruct us how to live in a manner that pleases Him, and ultimately, to reveal to us how we can be redeemed into everlasting life through our Lord and Savior Jesus Christ—the Lamb slain before the foundation of the world (Revelation 13:8).

APOLOGETICS BACKGROUND

As Christians, we believe by faith that God's Word is His true revelation to us and the foundation upon which we base our lives. Consequently, we have no need to "prove" its authenticity to others. We know that God's Holy Spirit prompted select men to write the words of Scripture, and these words are inspired by a God who cannot lie (Titus 1:2; Hebrews 6:18).

However, we would expect a book that came from God to meet certain criteria, including historical, prophetic, and scientific accuracy; a tone of authority; and a life-changing message.

Having said that, we can offer the following evidences to skeptics who ask us why we believe the Bible is the inspired, infallible, and inerrant Word of God.

- The Scriptures themselves proclaim to be God's Word and true as noted above (2 Timothy 3:16–17; 2 Peter 1:21; Hebrews 1:1–2).

- The Bible's message contains life-changing power. It transforms sinners into new creatures by the power of the Holy Spirit (2 Corinthians 5:17).

- Neither man nor Satan has been able to destroy God's Word—". . . but the word of our God stands forever" (Isaiah 40:8).

- Archaeological finds continue to confirm biblical truth. A renowned Jewish archaeologist once claimed, "It may be stated categorically that no archaeological discovery has ever controverted a Biblical reference." Nelson Glueck, *Rivers in the Desert* (New York: Farrar, Strous, and Cudahy, 1959), p. 136.

- The books of the Bible were written over a period of 1,600 years by 40 authors (from very different walks of life), writing in different places, times, moods, on different continents, in three languages, covering hundreds of controversial subjects—and yet they present absolute harmony from beginning to end.

- Old Testament passages give more than 50 prophecies of the birth, life, death, and Resurrection of Jesus Christ; and every prophecy (written more than 400 years before His birth) came true.

For those of us with faith to believe, these findings serve as confirmation that we worship a mighty God who does not change. He speaks to us through the consistently preserved Scriptures so we can know Him, His character, His purpose, and His plan to redeem a people to Himself for all eternity.

HISTORICAL BACKGROUND

The Bible is God's very Word to us. It will guide us through everything we encounter as we rely on it (Proverbs 30:5–6; Psalm 73:24, 119:133; 2 Peter 1:3). Because of this promise, His Word has been precious to believers throughout history. It has been copied and translated more than any other book, as it continues to guide people around the world.

The Greek Septuagint translation of the Old Testament was used, along with hand-written manuscripts of the New Testament gospels and epistles, in the early church. However, as the gospel spread, it became important to provide the Scriptures in other languages.

In 405 AD Jerome translated the Old and New Testaments from the original Hebrew and Greek into Latin. This became known as the Vulgate. This text was understood only by the elite, most of whom were priests. They were determined to keep the Bible from the ordinary people. Translation into common languages was discouraged and often severely prohibited.

Beginning in the fourteenth century, a new desperation developed to make the Scriptures available to the common man. For too long the Roman church had shackled the Scriptures, but they were about to be unleashed. God's Word would not be restrained— He intended for it to guide us through life.

The following represents some of the history of the Bible and when it became available.

- c. 1400 BC—The first written Word of God—the Ten Commandments
- c. 500 BC—Original Hebrew Manuscripts completed
- First century AD—All original Greek manuscripts of the New Testament were completed
- 1382—The Wycliffe Bible; a middle English translation from the Latin Vulgate
- 1526—The Tyndale Bible; a modern English translation

from the original Greek and Hebrew

- 1534—Martin Luther's German Bible is published from the Greek
- 1539—The Great Bible; the first English translation to be authorized for public use; commissioned by Henry VIII
- 1560—The Geneva Bible; the first study Bible published and the first English language Bible to include numbered verses to each chapter
- 1611—The King James Bible was printed and became the main Bible of the English language for the next 300 years

Today, the Bible continues to be the most translated book in the world. As of 2005, portions of the Bible had been translated into 2,400 languages. God is continuing to guide us with His Word as He continues to make His Word available to every tribe and tongue and people and nation (Revelation 5:9).

For more information on this topic, see the Online Resource Page.

Studying God's Word

How do these letters relate to our last lesson? O, I, and A

Take notes as you study the following passages.

2 Peter 1:19–21

Impossible for God?

Complete the Impossible for God? worksheet.

2 Timothy 3:16–17

God's Word in the Real World

1. What is the ultimate source of Scripture, and what passages can we use to support this idea?

2. How were the Scriptures delivered to us?

3. Why can we trust the Scriptures?

4. It is likely that you know people who doubt the truth of the Bible. They might say things like, "We can't trust the Bible, it was simply written by men." How would you go about discussing this idea with them?

5. Is it wise to leave the Bible out of the discussion about the Bible?

6. As we look to apply the four uses of Scripture we discussed, think about your personal devotion time or family Scripture reading. How could you put these four guiding principles into practice?

Prayer Requests

God Preserves His Word

4

Key Passages

- Luke 24:13–32; Jeremiah 36:1–4, 36:17–32

What You Will Learn

- How Jesus affirmed the authority of the Old Testament.

- When the Old Testament canon was written.

- Examples of the miraculous preservation of God's Word.

Lesson Overview

The Old Testament was recorded by various prophets over a 1,100-year period. God has preserved His Word through time, and we can trust it as an absolute authority.

Memory Verse

Psalm 19:7–9
The law of the Lord is perfect, converting the soul;
the testimony of the Lord is sure, making wise the simple;
the statutes of the Lord are right, rejoicing the heart;
the commandment of the Lord is pure, enlightening the eyes;
the fear of the Lord is clean, enduring forever;
the judgments of the Lord are true and righteous altogether.

Prepare to Learn

SCRIPTURAL BACKGROUND

The Old Testament begins God's Word—the history of the universe. It contains 39 books and tells us about ancient Israel and God's promise of the Messiah. This precious history has been revealed and preserved for us since the beginning of time.

One dramatic biblical episode of God preserving His Word begins in 2 Chronicles 34 during King Josiah's reign over Judah near the beginning of the seventh century BC. Josiah began a period of reformation in Judah. The people before him had completely turned away from God. But Josiah did what was right in the sight of the Lord and walked in His ways (2 Chronicles 34:2). The house of the Lord had been desecrated and Josiah commanded that it be repaired (2 Chronicles 34:8). It was during this restoration of the temple that Hilkiah the priest found the Book of the Law of the Lord given by Moses (2 Chronicles 34:14). When Josiah heard the Word of the Lord read, he was convicted of the idolatry and sin in the land. He tore his clothes in repentance (2 Chronicles 34:19). Because of Josiah's tender heart and humble spirit before God when he heard the words, God's judgment was withheld from Judah for the time (2 Chronicles 34:27–28).

However, when Josiah's son Jehoiakim became king, the people once again turned their backs on God and His Word. This is when the Word of the Lord came to the prophet Jeremiah (Jeremiah 36:1) and he was instructed by the Lord to write the words of judgment against Israel and Judah and all the nations (Jeremiah 36:2). Jeremiah dictated God's Word as Baruch wrote the scroll (Jeremiah 36:4). When the scroll was finished and read to King Jehoiakim, he was not afraid, repentant, or humble before the Lord as his father had been (Jeremiah 36:24). Instead, Jehoiakim destroyed the Word of God by casting the scroll into the fire piece by piece as it was being read (Jeremiah 36:22–23).

But was King Jehoiakim able to destroy God's Word even with fire? No. God will always preserve His Word and did so then. He called Jeremiah again and instructed that yet another scroll be written. Jeremiah took the scroll and gave it to Baruch the scribe, who wrote on it. It contained all the words (and more) of the book that Jehoiakim king of Judah had burned in the fire (Jeremiah 36:32).

God has always been and will always be faithful to preserve His Word. In the words of Isaiah the prophet, "The grass withers, the flower fades, but the word of our God stands forever" (Isaiah 40:8).

And in the words of the psalmist, "The entirety of Your Word is truth, and every one of Your righteous judgments endures forever" (Psalm 119:160).

APOLOGETICS BACKGROUND

You may encounter people who don't necessarily feel that the Old Testament is significant to today's culture. It is, however, the Word of God. And God has taken great strides to preserve it in order to reveal His truth and plan of redemption completely.

As we study our Lord's life recorded in the New Testament, we see one who relied on the truth and promises of the Old Testament. Indeed, Jesus placed such a high value on the inspired Word of God that even He—the very Son of God, the Messiah—willingly submitted Himself to its authority while on earth. He relied on it to resist the temptations of Satan (Matthew 4), and He read from it when He taught in the synagogues. In fact, He was reading from the Old Testament book of Isaiah when He proclaimed that He was the Messiah who fulfilled Isaiah's prophecy (Luke 4:16–21).

On the road to Emmaus (Luke 24:13), after His Resurrection, the Lord admonished His companions to believe the prophets (Luke 24:25). And as they walked, Jesus taught them from the Scriptures, beginning at the writings of Moses and all through the Prophets, the things concerning Him—that He was the one sent to redeem Israel (Luke 24:21). Jesus Christ studied, taught, obeyed, and lived the Scriptures of the Old Testament. Because He held them in such high regard, we should as well.

We do well to remember His words to Satan during His temptation: "It is written, 'Man does not live by bread alone, but by every word that proceeds from the mouth of God'" (Matthew 4:4).

HISTORICAL BACKGROUND

God has preserved His Word for thousands of years. And He has been gracious to leave historical evidence that confirms the Bible. We know that the ancient Hebrews relied on Scripture. They recognized the inspiration of certain texts and depended on them for wisdom.

The five books of Moses, beginning with Genesis, were written around 1500 BC and chronicle the history of the earth over the previous 2,500 years. After that, the remaining books were written by prophets and scribes. These holy men of God spoke as they were moved by the Holy Spirit (2 Peter 1:19–21). The words were recorded on scrolls and carefully transmitted through the generations with painstaking diligence to ensure their accuracy. The final record from the Old Testament prophets came at the hand of Malachi. His prophecy of the coming Prophet (Malachi 3–4) begins a period of 400 years of silence before John the Baptist proclaimed the arrival of Christ.

The Dead Sea Scrolls, discovered at Qumran in 1947, gave rise to additional confirmation of these ancient texts. This finding presented Old Testament manuscripts dated as early as 150 BC. These manuscripts were written nearly 1,000 years before other manuscripts already discovered and proved to be the same as those previously found.

For example, a copy of the book of Isaiah was part of the findings at Qumran dated about 150 BC. Prior to this, the oldest dated manuscript of the book of Isaiah was around AD 980. Yet when these two copies of Isaiah were compared, they were found to be 95 percent accurate to the Hebrew Bible.

This evidence of ancient Old Testament Hebrew texts together with the astounding number—more than 24,000—of partial and complete manuscript copies of the New Testament give us solid historical background to the reliability of the Bible. Biblical scholars have agreed that the number of manuscripts supporting the Bible provide unparalleled authentication of the original documents. In fact, the Bible has more documentation to verify it than any other book of antiquity that is commonly accepted.

For those of us with faith to believe, these findings serve as confirmation that we worship a mighty God who does not change. He speaks to us through the consistently preserved Scriptures so we can know Him, His character, His purpose, and His plan to redeem a people to Himself for all eternity.

For more information on this topic, see the Online Resource Page.

Studying God's Word

Which is more important: the Old Testament or the New Testament?

Take notes as you study the following passages.

Luke 24:13–32

Jeremiah 36:1–4, 36:17–19

Jeremiah 36:20–26

God's Word in the Real World

1. What can we learn from the way Jesus referred to the Old Testament?

2. How has God preserved the text of the Old Testament?

3. How does the encounter recorded in Luke 24 between the risen Jesus and His disciples along the road give you a clearer picture of the importance of the Old Testament?

4. What questions has this topic raised in your mind, and how might you go about answering those questions?

 ## Prayer Requests

God's Word Is Complete

5

Key Passages

- John 14:25–26, 21:24–25; Revelation 22:18–19

What You Will Learn

- The role of the Holy Spirit in writing the New Testament.
- The eyewitness nature of the New Testament writers.
- The approximate date of the closing of the canon of Scripture.

Lesson Overview

We know the New Testament is God's Word and that it is true. We realize that the Bible—both Old and New Testaments—contain the complete written Word of God from eyewitnesses to the events described.

Memory Verse

Psalm 19:7–9
The law of the Lord is perfect, converting the soul;
the testimony of the Lord is sure, making wise the simple;
the statutes of the Lord are right, rejoicing the heart;
the commandment of the Lord is pure, enlightening the eyes;
the fear of the Lord is clean, enduring forever;
the judgments of the Lord are true and righteous altogether.

📖 Prepare to Learn

SCRIPTURAL BACKGROUND

The Old Testament closed with a warning of judgment (Malachi 2:2) and the promise of a Messiah (Malachi 4:2). And then waiting. Four hundred years of silence from God. Silence until the fulfillment of the greatest event in history—the coming of the Messiah.

The New Testament—reflecting the fulfillment of the promised Messiah through Jesus Christ—was written primarily by the apostles. We find that Jesus empowered the apostles through the Holy Spirit to recall, write, and interpret the life, words, and deeds of Jesus. Jesus said in John 14:26, "But the Helper, the Holy Spirit, whom the Father will send in My name, He will teach you all things, and bring to your remembrance all things that I said to you." Jesus again promised His apostles a special revelation of truth through the Holy Spirit in John 16:13: "However, when He, the Spirit of truth, has come, He will guide you into all truth; for He will not speak on His own authority, but whatever He hears He will speak; and He will tell you things to come."

The Apostle John verifies himself as an eyewitness to the events he wrote about: "This is the disciple who testifies of these things, and wrote these things; and we know that his testimony is true" (John 21:24). And God officially warns against tampering with Scripture—admonishing that no words be added to or taken from this sacred book (Revelation 22:18–19). We can be confident that the writings of those empowered by Jesus Christ and the Holy Spirit are inspired, inerrant, and infallible.

As the New Testament letters began to be gathered and read throughout the church, we find evidence that they were already being included and described as "Scripture," including them as part of the established Old Testament canon. The Apostle Peter makes such a claim about Paul's writings in 2 Peter 3:15–16 when he puts Paul's epistles in the same category as the "rest of the Scriptures."

We can rest assured that the New Testament canon has now completed the Word of God. We are reminded of this truth through biblical, historical, and archaeological findings. Not only that, we know it is God's Word because as we read it we hear God's voice throughout every book—and as children of God we never tire of it. It is the Word of our Creator God—revealing the divine power that allows us everything needed to live a life of godliness through the knowledge of God and of Jesus our Lord (2 Peter 1:3).

APOLOGETICS BACKGROUND

In His divine providence, God, not man, has determined through the Holy Spirit the books that make up the Bible. The early church, shortly after Christ's death and Resurrection, had no discussion about what made a book equal to the Old Testament Scriptures. It was universally accepted that if a letter came from Peter or Paul, it was deemed Scripture.

However, it wasn't long before people began to add their own letters, thoughts, ideas, and gospels—desiring to fill in the gaps with what they believed should be included. Because of this, during the first 200 years of church history, certain questions were adopted to serve as the litmus test for the books added to the Bible. All of the books of the Bible regarded as Scripture fulfill these requirements.

- Was the book or letter written by an apostle or under the direction of an apostle?

- Did the writing resound with the truth of God? Did it speak with the voice of authority as the Word of God and not the words of men?

- Were these writings used from the earliest of times? Attempts to include other writings from much later dates have been made. They have been rejected because the material is too new to have been apostolic.

- Did most churches accept these writings as the New Testament canon? Before the middle of the first century, 20 of the 27 books of the New Testament were universally accepted. And only a few churches questioned the other books.

- Did the writings conform to what the church taught? Because there was general agreement as to what the Christian message actually was, this question ruled out false teachings attempting to taint the truth.

Still today we see how people attack the authenticity and reliability of the Scriptures. We must be on our guard against such attacks—and confidently turn to the Word of God to weigh the truth of any claim.

HISTORICAL BACKGROUND

The Bible is increasingly regarded as not relevant due to the apathy of our culture toward things of God and the authority of His Word. Consequently, we hear very little about the history of the Bible. As we take a quick look at the books of the New Testament below, keep in mind that these books stood the litmus test based on the questions mentioned above as they were included in the canon of the New Testament.

- The Gospels—Matthew, Mark, Luke, and John provide accounts of Jesus's life, death, and Resurrection during his three-year ministry. Matthew, Mark, and Luke were written between AD 55–68; John was probably written in the 90s.

- The book of Acts—This is an account of the history of the early church and the spread of Christianity after Christ's Resurrection. Acts was written by Luke in the mid-60s.

- The Pauline epistles—Romans, 1 & 2 Corinthians, Galatians, Ephesians, Philippians, Colossians, 1 & 2 Thessalonians, 1 & 2 Timothy, Titus, and Philemon are 13 pastoral letters written by Paul as he endeavored to grow Christ's church in truth and sound doctrine. These letters were written between AD 51 and 65.

- The general epistles— Hebrews, James, 1 & 2 Peter, 1, 2, & 3 John, and Jude are letters written to believers by five different people. They include doctrinal and practical advice and were sent out to churches. These letters were written from the late-40s (James's letter) to the 90s (John's letters).

Most of the New Testament books were added to the Old Testament Scriptures by the early church and were considered the complete inspired canon around AD 150—this is called the Muratorian canon. However, due to false teachers and attempts to change this compilation, other councils—general meetings of the Christian church—met to eliminate the confusion and bring unity to the church. The Council of Carthage in 397 finally affirmed publicly that the 66 books we have today were the divinely inspired Word of God—not to be added to or taken from (Proverbs 30:5–6).

For more information on this topic, see the Online Resource Page.

 Studying God's Word

Why are there exactly 27 books in the New Testament?

Take notes as you study the following passages.

John 14:25–26

John 21:24–25

A Common Thread

Complete the A Common Thread worksheet.

Revelation 22:18–19

God's Word in the Real World

1. How was the Holy Spirit involved in the recording of the New Testament?

2. What common thread do we see with all of the writers of the New Testament?

3. How do we respond to claims that the New Testament was written hundreds of years after the lives of the apostles?

4. How does what we have discussed today challenge ideas that you may have had about the New Testament?

5. What about today's lesson gives you encouragement or assurance about your faith?

Prayer Requests

Don't Change God's Word

6

Key Passages

- Deuteronomy 18:20–22; Revelation 22:18–19; Galatians 1:6–9

What You Will Learn

- How to differentiate between those who speak for God and those who are false prophets.
- Examples of religions that have added to or taken away from the Bible.

Lesson Overview

Despite claims of many modern prophets, the sixty-six books of the Bible remain the only written words that have come from God. The Bible must be the absolute authority to compare every thought against.

Memory Verse

Psalm 19:7–9
The law of the Lord is perfect, converting the soul;
the testimony of the Lord is sure, making wise the simple;
the statutes of the Lord are right, rejoicing the heart;
the commandment of the Lord is pure, enlightening the eyes;
the fear of the Lord is clean, enduring forever;
the judgments of the Lord are true and righteous altogether.

📖 Prepare to Learn

SCRIPTURAL BACKGROUND

"Now the serpent was more cunning than any beast of the field . . . . And he said to the woman, "Has God indeed said, 'You shall not eat of every tree in the garden'?" (Genesis 3:1). Just as Satan cast doubt on God's Word in the very beginning, the Word of God has been questioned, denied, changed, added to, and misinterpreted throughout history.

We are called to search the Scriptures to discover the truth— to be Bereans (see Acts 17:10–11). We can have confidence and trust in God's Word as our final authority, and be careful to obey it.

Deuteronomy 4:2—"You shall not add to the word which I command you, nor take from it, that you may keep the commandments of the Lord your God which I command you."

Deuteronomy 12:32—"Whatever I command you, be careful to observe it; you shall not add to it nor take away from it."

Deuteronomy 18:20–22— "But the prophet who presumes to speak a word in My name, which I have not commanded him to speak, or who speaks in the name of other gods, that prophet shall die. And if you say in your heart, 'How shall we know the word which the Lord has not spoken?'— when a prophet speaks in the name of the Lord, if the thing does not happen or come to pass, that is the thing which the Lord has not spoken; the prophet has spoken it presumptuously; you shall not be afraid of him."

Galatians 1:6–9—"I marvel that you are turning away so soon from Him who called you in the grace of Christ, to a different gospel, which is not another; but there are some who trouble you and want to pervert the gospel of Christ. But even if we, or an angel from heaven, preach any other gospel to you than what we have preached to you, let him be accursed. As we have said before, so now I say again, if anyone preaches any other gospel to you than what you have received, let him be accursed."

And as we reach the Bible's final chapter, we are given God's assurance that it is complete as He warns that it must not be changed in any way.

Revelation 22:18–19—"For I testify to everyone who hears the words of the prophecy of this book: If anyone adds to these things, God will add to him the plagues that are written in this book; and if anyone takes away from the words of the book of this prophecy, God shall take away his part from the Book of Life, from the holy city, and from the things which are written in this book."

APOLOGETICS BACKGROUND

Tolerance—it's a word we often hear in this culture. The attitude today is to be open-minded, accept everyone, be careful not to offend anyone, and accept all religions as equally true. If it works for you—it works! This is not an accurate understanding of tolerance, but a twisted view that comes from the post-modern mindset where people can construct their own truth. Real tolerance involves understanding the positions of others, knowing why you disagree, living alongside them, and confronting their false ideas with biblical truth. If we are not convinced that someone is wrong, why would we need to tolerate their different views?

As Christians, we are called to follow the example of Jesus Christ, who was not tolerant of false religions, but stood on the truth of God's Word (e.g., John 3:34, 14:6, 17:3).

Is the Bible the only Word of God? Be assured, God's Word needs no proof. God begins with the presumption that He exists (Genesis 1:1) and follows up with many texts that authenticate His Word (e.g., Proverbs 30:5; Psalm 119:160; John 17:17). He does, however, warn us against succumbing to empty deceit, traditions of men, and the principles of the world that are not of Christ (Colossians 2:8).

With this in mind let's take a look at how some false religions blatantly deny the truth of God and the work of Jesus Christ.

We need to be very aware that there are many false teachings in the world today. And only God's Word provides us with the information we need to reveal them for what they are. The Bible is the only Word of God.

	Bible	Islam	Mormonism	Jehovah's Witnesses
View of Origins	God created all things in six 24-hour days, about 6,000 years ago. All creatures, including man, were created after their own kinds. Sin, disease, sickness, and death were not part of this creation. They came as a result of the Fall.	The Koran teaches that Allah created all things, but it contradicts itself on the number of days. It also teaches that the first man and woman were created in Paradise but were later banished to earth after the fall into sin.	God created man physically after He created the earth. However, we had a pre-earth life, in which we existed as God's "spirit children."	The Watchtower Society teaches that each of the six creative days of God in Genesis 1 was 7,000 years long and that the universe is billions of years old.
View of Christ	Jesus is the only begotten Son of God, who became man to live a perfect life, to be mankind's substitute on the Cross, and to rise from the dead, defeating death.	Allah (God) created Jesus and appointed Him to be a messenger to the Jewish people. The Koran teaches that Jesus was sinless but that He was not God, and that He did not die on the Cross.	Jesus is the spirit-brother to every man and even Satan. Jesus is one of an endless number of gods and is a being separate from the Heavenly Father.	Jesus is the Son of God but He is a created being. Christ existed in a pre-human state as the Archangel Michael. Jesus died at His crucifixion and was resurrected as an invisible, non-material, glorious, spirit creature.

	Bible	Islam	Mormonism	Jehovah's Witnesses
Sin and Salvation	Every person has sinned and fallen short of the glory of God. Salvation is by grace through faith in Christ and His redeeming work on the Cross.	Salvation is possible after adherence to the Koran, as well as performing the five pillars of the Islamic faith. But even then, salvation is not guaranteed.	Sin was part of God's plan because without it mankind could not progress to become like God, know joy, or have children. Salvation is a combination of faith and works.	Human nature is universally sinful, because all humans inherit the original sin of Adam and Eve. Salvation comes by placing faith in Christ's sacrifice, being baptized as a Witness, and doing good works.
Life after Death	Mankind will live forever either in heaven or in hell. The only way for us to get to heaven is through faith in Christ.	Allah sends both righteous and unrighteous to hell unless they die in a holy war. But if their good works outweigh their bad, they should be admitted into Paradise. Paradise is only guaranteed to those who die in jihad (holy war).	Even after death, everyone has an opportunity to respond to the gospel. Heaven has three levels, and those who attain the highest level become gods, ruling and populating their own universe.	There is no eternal hell; this is a false concept created by Satan to turn people away from belief in Jehovah. Unbelievers cease to exist at death (annihilation), while believers remain in death until the resurrection. Only 144,000 will go to heaven, while the rest will live in an earthly paradise.

HISTORICAL BACKGROUND

God presumed His existence and felt no need to prove it. His Word commences with, "In the beginning, God . . ." (Genesis 1:1), and that is how our history started.

Believers who have gone before us have demonstrated how much the Bible meant to them. They were willing to go to great sacrifice in order to spread the Word throughout the world in common languages because they knew it to be the only Word of God.

Consider John Wycliffe who was born in England in 1324. In those days, church leaders purposely kept ordinary people from the Scriptures. John Wycliffe declared that God's Word is for all people and he began a quest to produce the Scriptures in common English—handwritten from the Latin translations then available. These translations had to be read in secret and Wycliffe suffered persecution all of his life for his efforts.

John Huss, born in 1369 in Scotland, was another of God's servants. John Huss was intent on maintaining the Word of God as the authority over Christian doctrine, and he spoke boldly and courageously against the compromises he saw in the church such as altering the Lord's Supper and selling indulgences. As a result, he was burned at the stake—giving his life so the Word of God might remain the pure standard for the church.

German believers experienced similar persecution. When Martin Luther was born in 1483, the Bible was a very rare book and practically unknown. As he grew, so did his love for the Bible, God, and truth. Luther was aware that there were grave and unbiblical injustices in the church and God stirred his soul to action. On October 31, 1517, he posted his complaints against the church authorities—jeopardizing his life to defend the Bible as the only Word of God.

At the time Luther was translating God's Word into German, God also stirred William Tyndale (1483–1536) to desire that the Word be available in the English language. This was a terrible time in England and Tyndale's spirit, boldness, and faithfulness to God's Word put his life in constant danger. Yet he pursued his God-given vocation and eventually did complete a translation of the New Testament—the first translation into English from the original Greek. Ultimately, God's will was for Tyndale to die a martyr's death.

These are but a few of the saints who have gone before us to preserve, protect, and provide the Word of God. It is the only Word of God—and around the world people are still giving up their lives to honor its integrity.

For more information on this topic, see the Online Resource Page.

 ## Studying God's Word

How do you know whether or not the Book of Mormon is a revelation from God?

Take notes as you study the following passages.

Deuteronomy 18:20–22

Revelation 22:18–19

A Different Gospel

Complete the A Different Gospel worksheet.

 ## God's Word in the Real World

1. How would you respond if someone says that they follow a different prophet who has heard from God, and that the Bible needs to be reinterpreted correctly for us to understand it?

2. How do we guard against being influenced by language that sounds biblical but carries different definitions?

3. If a prophet claims to be speaking for God but is found to be a false prophet, what/who is the source of the prophecies?

4. Why is it important to be able to discern who false prophets are?

Prayer Requests

7

Starting with Scripture

Key Passages

- 1 Peter 3:14–17; 2 Corinthians 10:1–6; Acts 17; Proverbs 26:4–5

What You Will Learn

- To distinguish between evidential and presuppositional apologetic approaches.
- How to explain the "Don't Answer-Answer" apologetic strategy.
- That it is the Holy Spirit who brings conviction leading to salvation.

Lesson Overview

Apologetics is the defense of the Christian's hope in Christ. All believers are called to give a reason for the hope they have. We should unashamedly use the Bible to make our defense.

Memory Verse

Psalm 19:7–9
The law of the Lord is perfect, converting the soul;
the testimony of the Lord is sure, making wise the simple;
the statutes of the Lord are right, rejoicing the heart;
the commandment of the Lord is pure, enlightening the eyes;
the fear of the Lord is clean, enduring forever;
the judgments of the Lord are true and righteous altogether.

📖 Prepare to Learn

SCRIPTURAL BACKGROUND

The Bible is the only revealed Word of God. We trust that it contains truth from the Creator of the universe. When God created, He made a universe that was perfect, but that perfection was short lived. The Fall of mankind into sin is chronicled in Genesis 3. Sin's impact in the world is so extensive that it has even corrupted the thinking process. Man is not inclined toward God but has actually set his mind against God (Romans 8:5–8). The natural man's mind cannot understand spiritual things because the Holy Spirit is not present within him (1 Corinthians 2:14). It is extremely important that we keep this in mind as we seek to share the truths of Scriptures with people living in a fallen state.

Scripture tells us that we are called to share the gospel with the world (Matthew 28:19–20), to defend the faith and hope we have in Christ (1 Peter 3:15), and attack the arguments made against God (2 Corinthians 10:1–6). We are to speak words of truth to a lost world, but it is not our words that bring about salvation—it is the Holy Spirit. Jesus told His disciples that the Helper would come to convict the world of sin (John 16:7–11). It is also the Spirit who brings new life as someone repents and puts his trust in Christ (John 3:5–8). While Christians are charged with speaking the words of life, the Holy Spirit is solely responsible for enabling the sinner to repent and believe in Christ. We should not place the burden of conversion on ourselves—it is the work of God the Spirit.

We might present piles of evidence and an articulate case for the existence of God, but the unbelieving mind is blind to the spiritual truths we are proclaiming, and they will reject the truth. There are many examples of people rejecting the evidence that was set right before them. This is because everyone interprets evidence in light of his or her worldview. Many people saw Jesus raise Lazarus from the dead. Many believed in Him, but some went away in unbelief (John 11:43–48). As Jesus explained the account of the rich man and Lazarus, He made it clear through Abraham's words that even if one rises from the dead, people would not believe. Abraham appealed to Moses and the prophets (an allusion to the Scriptures) as the source of truth for the living to look to (Luke 16:19–31). Scripture contains the words of eternal life. Even after Christ's resurrection and appearance, some doubted (Matthew 28:17). What makes us think that our arguments should be placed above the truths of Scripture as we defend the faith?

As we look for a model for defending the faith, we should appeal to the Bible. Paul used Scripture. Peter used Scripture. Jesus used Scripture. Even when addressing the pagans at the Areopagus, Paul presented biblical doctrines of God as the Creator as the very foundation of his argument. He then moved directly to a call to repentance and the Resurrection of Christ (Acts 17:19–34). He did not shy away from presenting biblical truths in the face of a pagan audience—he used Scripture from the beginning of his argument. We would do well to follow his example.

APOLOGETICS BACKGROUND

Many people have a misunderstanding of Christian apologetics. This curriculum is different from most in that it specifically intends to weave apologetic principles into the concepts being studied. Apologists are not interested in providing "I'm sorry that . . ." statements about biblical beliefs. Our idea of apologetics comes from 1 Peter 3:15 where believers are called to "always be ready to give a defense" for the hope they have in Christ. We take the term apologetics from the Greek word *apologia*—a reasoned defense of the hope we have. Likewise, Paul calls believers to tear down strongholds and cast down arguments that are set forth against God (2 Corinthians 10:1–6).

Knowing that we are to be prepared to give a defense for our faith, we must consider how we give that defense. There are many different apologetic methods, but we want to make sure that the method we employ comes from Scripture. The many approaches fall into two basic camps: evidential and presuppositional. The evidential approach uses probabilities and natural revelation to attempt to persuade the unbeliever that there is a god and that the most reasonable answer to who that god is can be found in the Bible. This is the approach of the Intelligent Design Movement, classical apologetics, and various other forms that make the initial arguments without calling on Scripture.

The presuppositional approach is not against the use of evidence, as is commonly claimed, but starts with the assumption that the Bible is true. Rather than setting the Bible aside because the unbeliever doesn't accept its truthfulness, the Bible is put forward as the standard of truth and arguments are made from that truth. Rather than attempting to reason to God, presuppositional apologetics reasons from God's Word. Romans 1 makes it clear that all people know that God exists from the creation that surrounds them. If the biblical God did not exist, even making an argument would be impossible. Only the biblical God can explain the existence of natural laws, logic, and absolute morality.

The basic concept of this apologetic method is found in Proverbs 26:4–5, which says, "Do not answer a fool according to his folly, lest you also be like him. Answer a fool according to his folly, lest he be wise in his own eyes."

On the surface, these verses seem to contradict one another. However, they actually offer a biblical method for apologetics. This has been framed by Dr. Jason Lisle, a scientist and apologist, as the "Don't Answer–Answer" strategy: Don't accept the unbiblical reasoning of an unbeliever lest you think like him; answer the unbeliever using his own philosophy (worldview) and show him how it leads to foolishness.

When defending the faith, we must draw attention to the heart of the matter—the different starting points of the arguments. Remember that everyone looks at the world through a set of lenses—a worldview. We must not accept the idea that there is neutral ground to ague from. We must rely on Scripture as our anchor when defending the faith.

Please consider watching the video *The Ultimate Proof of Creation*, which is available from the Online Resource Page, for more explanation of this topic. A portion of this video will be used in this lesson.

HISTORICAL BACKGROUND

From its very beginning, the church has given a defense for the hope that believers have in Christ. Peter stood among the crowds on the Day of Pentecost and from Scripture boldly defended what was happening among them (Acts 2:14–41). Stephen presents another example, giving a defense before the council who would condemn him to death. Paul also gave a defense from Scripture as he traveled through Europe and reasoned in the synagogues and marketplaces. All of these men used Scripture as the foundation for their defense of the faith—their apologetic.

As the church grew, many great men rose up to defend the faith. Justin Martyr, Tertullian, Irenaeus, Thomas Aquinas, Jerome, and many others wrote in defense of the faith; however, they used different forms of argument. Some started from nature, attempting to demonstrate that God was necessary. Some began from the philosophy of causes (cosmological argument); some from apparent design and purpose in the universe (teleology); and others from various points of philosophy. Many abandoned the authority of Scripture in their arguments.

Although many of those arguments have merit, they cannot be divorced from the truths of Scripture. We must start with the presupposition of God's Word as the ultimate truth. If we only convince someone that there is a god, we have failed to share the truth of Scripture. We must communicate who God is and what He has done through Christ—truths found only in the Bible.

For more information on this topic, see the Online Resource Page.

Studying God's Word

Circle the right answer. The goal of Christian apologetics is to:

a) persuade people to believe in the Bible.

b) apologize for the wacky things Christians believe.

c) persuade people to believe in Christ.

d) give a reasoned defense for Christian beliefs.

Take notes as you study the following passages.

1 Peter 3:14–17

Acts 17

Foolproof Apologetics Video Notes

"NEUTRAL GROUND"

Why should we never leave the Bible out of the argument?

"DON'T ANSWER–ANSWER"

Summarize the "Don't Answer–Answer" strategy.

_____

_____

_____

_____

 ## God's Word in the Real World

1. What is the basic goal of apologetics?

2. What are the two basic approaches to apologetics and how are they different?

3. Does the idea that we are called to always be ready to give a defense for our faith challenge you in any way?

4. How does understanding the role of the Holy Spirit in apologetics and evangelism give you a degree of relief?

5. How would you respond to someone who asked you a question that you didn't know the answer to?

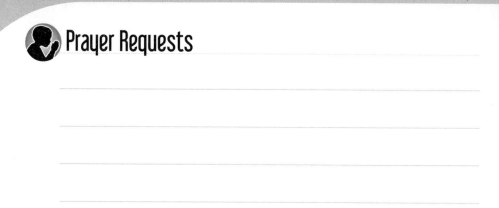

Prayer Requests

How Do I Know God Exists?

8

Key Passages

- Genesis 1:1; Exodus 3:13–15; John 18:1–6

What You Will Learn

- Three reasons, from Scripture and the realm of experience, for the existence of the biblical God.

- That God exists outside time and He is the Creator of everything, including time.

- The difference between the presuppositional and evidential approaches of confirming God's existence.

Lesson Overview

Since the Bible presupposes the existence of God, the writers did not seek to prove His existence. A universe without the biblical God is impossible.

Memory Verse

Psalm 119:89–90
Forever, O Lord, Your word is settled in heaven. Your faithfulness endures to all generations; You established the earth, and it abides.

Prepare to Learn

SCRIPTURAL BACKGROUND

"How do I know God exists?" This is a question that has been and will be debated as long as sinners occupy the earth. First of all, as Christians who walk by faith and not by sight (2 Corinthians 5:7), we do not need to prove the existence of God. The Bible says that we accept God by faith—that we *believe* that He exists and that He rewards those who earnestly seek Him (Hebrews 11:6). Because the Bible is our basis for all we believe, we believe in God as presented in the Bible.

God's Word begins with the proclamation that He and He alone existed from eternity past: "In the beginning God . . ." (Genesis 1:1). If He had wanted to prove Himself to the world in a way our minds could grasp, He could have done that. God saw no need to explain further. Belief in Him as the one true God comes by faith and trust in Him and His Word.

Genesis 1 continues to describe this God who spoke the entire universe into existence. The order we see in creation—from the stars, solar systems, animal and plant life, to the natural laws of gravity, motion, and thermo-dynamics—gives evidence of an omnipotent Creator. There is no other explanation. The universe is not a result of random chance. It was created by one who was not created. There had to be someone who never came into being. There had to be a Creator. God—the one true God—is that Creator, who was and is and is to come (Revelation 4:8).

As we look to the Scriptures, we see that God described Himself to Moses as "I AM WHO I AM," which essentially means: *the one who is and will be* (Exodus 3:13–14). The eternal, self-existent nature of God is revealed through His Word and simply assumed. Through the inspiration of the Holy Spirit, again, John records that the Lord is the Alpha and the Omega, the Beginning and the End, who is and who was and who is to come, the Almighty (Revelation 1:8). What more do we need? This describes the only, holy, omnipotent, omniscient God of the universe—who was and is and always will be. He is not bound by time as we know it. He created time in the beginning (Genesis 1:1).

God in His mercy has also specifically revealed Himself through His incredible creation. "The heavens declare the glory of God, and the firmament shows His handiwork" (Psalm 19:1). And the Apostle Paul tells us that since the creation of the world, God's invisible attributes have been seen through creation, revealing His eternal power and Godhead—leaving those who do not believe in Him without excuse (Romans 1:18–21). God does indeed exist. His existence is confirmed in Scripture and through His creation—and the wrath of God will be revealed from heaven against all who suppress the truth of His existence in unrighteousness.

APOLOGETICS BACKGROUND

Look around you; what do you see? An amazingly designed universe—from the single cell to the vast and immeasurable solar system. And yet the debate for a Creator of such things rages. We can rest in God's Word, "In the beginning God . . ." (Genesis 1:1). We know that if something exists, it was somehow created into being. And as Christians we know who that Creator was. But what of folks who state there was no Creator—it all began with a bang, a very "big bang," one that allegedly occurred billions of years ago in one tiny speck of mass and energy, a speck that would one day become everything we see today?

This story of the big bang originated with an attempt to completely discount the Bible and its account of our Creator God. Christians who buy into it need to understand the atheistic beginnings of this secular story and why it cannot be "added" to the biblical account of Genesis 1 without destroying the Bible's integrity.

From a practical standpoint, have you ever blown something up and then observed the pieces re-assembling into a complex . . . anything? No, when buildings are demolished, they pretty much end up in a heap of debris with no order or design. And yet, the big bang proposed by some has supposedly produced intricate life and more. In fact, this notion claims that out of a random explosion and expansion of matter billions of years ago, life in its complexity and beauty—from the human body to the ant, from the wonder of the solar system to the universe beyond—has been organized and arranged into the complex world we live in today by nothing more than random, natural processes.

But, we know that the very existence of design, order, natural laws, and principles in the universe demands that there was a Creator—an Organizer, a Designer—not a big bang. That Creator can only be the one true Creator God. The only one who has declared Himself the Creator (Genesis 1), and the only one who proclaims that He Himself is sustaining the universe—personally maintaining life and upholding all things by the word of His power (Colossians 1:17; Hebrews 1:3). This Creator, our God, is truly worthy to receive glory and honor and power—for He created all things, and by His will they exist and were created (Revelation 4:11)!

HISTORICAL BACKGROUND

The serpent asked, "Has God indeed said, 'You shall not eat of every tree of the garden'?" (Genesis 3:1). And when Adam and Eve succumbed to this deception, that's when sin, deceit, pride, evil, hatred, death, and suffering entered the world. From the very beginning, people have wanted to be their own gods—and Satan is the primary encourager of this. The God of the Bible demands obedience, reverence, and accountability. God will one day judge the world in righteousness (Psalm 96:13).

Those who believe God's Word know this to be true—we believe God exists. However, many doubt the very existence of God. These atheists boldly turn from the greatest commandment—"You shall have no other gods before Me" (Exodus 20:3)—to pursue the imaginings of their own minds. Our culture has been shaped by these people who claim there is no God. We'll look at a few of them here.

Charles Darwin, the father of evolution, although not a proclaimed atheist, was influenced immensely by his atheist grandfather Erasmus. Darwin's idea of evolution has changed the course of human history and is one of the greatest attacks on the Word of God in our modern time.

Karl Marx, referred to by some as the greatest thinker in all of history, once stated that religion is the opiate of the masses—impotence of the human mind to deal with occurrences it cannot understand.

Sigmund Freud, considered by some as psychology's most famous figure, believed that religion was nothing more than an expression of underlying psychological neuroses and distress.

More recently, Madalyn Murray O'Hair was instrumental in removing prayer from the public schools in 1963. She believed that religion has caused more misery to all of mankind in every stage of human history than any other single idea.

And today we have those who are referred to as the "new atheists"—men such as Richard Dawkins, Christopher Hitchens, and Sam Harris—and they are aggressively going after your children, your liberties, and your faith! Dawkins, a scientist and an active leader in this movement, believes that one of the things wrong with religion is that it teaches us to be satisfied with answers that are not answers at all. These men and others have accused Christians of "child abuse" for teaching their children the Bible and passing on their faith.

The worldview of these atheists is dangerous to our culture. However, as Christians we are confident in the promises of the Word of God. We must not lose heart. We must be committed to proclaiming the gospel of Jesus Christ and enthused about keeping God on His throne as Sovereign Creator and Sustainer of all (Colossians 1:17). God has assured us that His Word is settled forever and His faithfulness will endure to all generations (Psalm 119:89–90).

For more information on this topic, see the Online Resource Page.

Studying God's Word

How do we prove God exists?

Take notes as you study the following passages.

Genesis 1:1

Exodus 3:13–15

John 18:1–6

1 Peter 1:20

God's Word in the Real World

1. What does Scripture have to say about the believer's responsibility for sharing their faith?

2. If someone asks you how you know God exists, how would you respond?

3. What is the proper role of evidence in our apologetics?

4. Is an evidence-first approach to evangelism/apologetics ever useful?

 # Prayer Requests

9

What Is God Like?

Key Passages

- Exodus 34:4–8; 1 John 4:9–11; Psalm 90:1–4

What You Will Learn

- That we must start with the Bible as our starting point to understand what God is like.

- Seven attributes of God found in Scripture.

Lesson Overview

God's attributes are demonstrated in direct claims from Scripture and are also understood from the way God interacts with His creation. We must use the Bible in order to understand God.

Memory Verse

Psalm 119:89–90
Forever, O Lord, Your word is settled in heaven. Your faithfulness endures to all generations; You established the earth, and it abides.

Prepare to Learn

SCRIPTURAL BACKGROUND

What is God like? How can we presume to answer this question? Our God is nothing but incomprehensible—He can never be fully understood. In fact, as believers we anticipate an eternity of discovering new things about Him.

David said of Him, "Great is the Lord, and greatly to be praised; and His greatness is unsearchable" (Psalm 145:3). And, "Yours, O Lord, is the greatness, the power and the glory, the victory and the majesty; for all that is in heaven and in earth is Yours; Yours is the kingdom, O Lord, and You are exalted as head over all" (1 Chronicles 29:11). We can't say it any better than the Apostle Paul, "Oh, the depth of the riches both of the wisdom and knowledge of God! How unsearchable are His judgments and His ways past finding out" (Romans 11:33)! The glimpses of God we observe from His Word are far, far from complete.

Question 4 of the historic Westminster Catechism, penned in the 1640s asks, "What is God?" The answer?

God is Spirit (John 4:24), infinite (Jeremiah 23:24), eternal (Psalm 90:2), and unchangeable (Malachi 3:6), in His being (James 1:17), wisdom (Psalm 147:5), power (Revelation 19:6), holiness (1 Samuel 2:2), justice (Psalm 7:11), goodness (Psalm 107:8), and truth (Deuteronomy 32:4).

When the Lord descended in the cloud to speak with Moses, He gave testimony to His very character—He proclaimed Himself as merciful, gracious, long-suffering, abundant in goodness, always truthful, forgiving, and, at the same time, just—not clearing the guilty (Exodus 34:6–7).

Knowing God and knowing that He is perfect in every one of His attributes is imperative to maturing in the Christian faith. That is why we have incorporated teaching these attributes as part of this Bible curriculum. So the next generation will know, love, honor, revere, and fear the God of all creation!

APOLOGETICS BACKGROUND

Because there is no way to comprehend the vast depth of our holy God, we are at risk of conjuring up in our minds what we want Him to be. This is not acceptable. We can only begin to know who God is by the revelation of His Word.

God is all-loving (1 John 4:7–21). But this attribute has been skewed by many Christians and non-Christians alike. The tendency of many is to make God a type of butler—one who waits at our beck and call and exists in order to answer our demands for blessing and comfort. We seldom witness the awe and wonder His very name deserves in our world today.

This attitude reeks of misunderstanding the holiness of God. His holiness demands that He despise each and every sin committed. Knowing His frightful hatred for sin should bring us to a reverent and godly fear of the one who is a consuming fire (Hebrews 12:28–29). Only true fear of the Lord will bring knowledge (Proverbs 1:7).

It is not until we fear God for who He is that we will humbly begin to understand the depths of His love—which is beyond all love. It is amazing that He would love us so much to send His only Son to die a horrible death in order to provide forgiveness to all who would believe (John 3:16). Because of the depth of His love, He was willing to offer the life of the one who committed no sin, yet was made sin for us—despicable sinners—so that we could be made the righteousness of God (Romans 5:8; 2 Corinthians 5:21).

God is love, yes. But His definition of love goes way beyond the scope of ours. His love is demonstrated in the gospel—that Christ died for our sins according to the Scriptures, He was buried, and He rose again the third day (1 Corinthians 15:3–4). It is only through our sincere and reverent fear for the holy, sinless God

that His amazing love through the free gift of salvation can finally be appreciated.

HISTORICAL BACKGROUND

What is God like? We have settled the question that He is beyond explanation—but His Word does give us a hint of the vast dimension of His character.

Historically, this is what we know. In the beginning, when God created Adam and Eve in the very good world, they saw God clearly. Scripture tells us that God talked with Adam and Eve, and He walked with them in the garden (Genesis 3:8). It is understood that before their disobedience, Adam and Eve enjoyed sweet fellowship with their Creator. They knew what God was like.

But sin entered the world through one man's disobedience (Romans 5:19). They were no longer welcome to walk with God (Genesis 3:23–24) because God cannot dwell with evil or wickedness (Psalm 5:4). Since then, man has wondered about God but has not been allowed to see Him as Adam and Eve did.

Moses was once bold enough to ask to see more of God (Exodus 33:18). Although God is compassionate and gracious, He would not allow Moses to see His face lest Moses die. God instructed Moses to hide in the cleft of the rock while His glory passed by (Exodus 33:22–23).

In Jesus, we know of God yet have not seen Him; "No

one has seen God at any time. The only begotten Son, who is in the bosom of the Father, He has declared Him" (John 1:18). And Paul recorded to Timothy, "[God] who alone has immortality, dwelling in unapproachable light, whom no man has seen or can see, to whom be honor and everlasting power. Amen" (1 Timothy 6:16). So for now, God keeps Himself in unapproachable light—masked to us until He is ready to be revealed.

But what a day that will be when His children will be like Him for they will see Him as He is (1 John 3:2)! How we long for the day we will once again see God, talk with Him, and enjoy the fellowship that was originally intended—but broken because of sin. "Blessed be the God and Father of our Lord Jesus Christ, who according to His abundant mercy has begotten us again to a living hope" (1 Peter 1:3).

For more information on this topic, see the Online Resource Page.

Studying God's Word

What is God like?

Take notes as you study the following passages.

Exodus 34:4-8

1 John 4:9-11

Psalm 90:1-4

God's Word in the Real World

Meditate on God's Attributes and take time to praise Him for who He is.

Prayer Requests

10
The Trinity

Key Passages

- Genesis 1:1–3; Psalm 33:6; John 1:1–5;
  Isaiah 44:23–24; Colossians 1:15–17;
  Psalm 104:30; Matthew 3:13–17

What You Will Learn

- Biblical support for the Trinity.

- The differences between the orthodox
  Christian view of the Trinity and views
  historically identified as heresies.

Lesson Overview

Even though the word *Trinity* is not found in the Bible, it accurately explains the triune nature of God as presented in Scripture.

Memory Verse

Psalm 119:89–90
Forever, O Lord, Your word is settled in heaven. Your faithfulness endures to all generations; You established the earth, and it abides.

📖 Prepare to Learn

SCRIPTURAL BACKGROUND

The word *Trinity* is not found in Scripture, but the concept of the Trinity is clear in its accounts. It is an important doctrine of the Christian faith, advocating that God eternally exists as three Persons. The Father is God, the Son is God, and the Holy Spirit is God—but there is only one God. Because of our finite minds, this concept is impossible to fully understand and/or explain. Let's consider a few things.

There is only one God. "I am the Lord and there is no other; there is no God besides Me" (Isaiah 45:5). See also Isaiah 46:9; Galatians 3:20; 1 Corinthians 8:5–6.

All three Persons of the Trinity—the Father, Son, and Holy Spirit—are called God. In Christ dwells all the fullness of the Godhead bodily (Colossian 2:9). The Holy Spirit and God are both referred to as God (Acts 5:3–4).

All three Persons of the Trinity are eternal. God is from everlasting to everlasting (Psalm 90:2). The throne of the Son is forever and ever (Hebrews 1:8). The Spirit, too, is eternal (Hebrews 9:14).

All three Persons of the Trinity are Creator; let's expound a bit here using the background Scriptures listed above.

Genesis 1:1–3 clearly references that God and the Spirit of God were present at creation.

John 1:1–5 brings Christ—the second Person of the Trinity—into the picture at creation. He was in the beginning with God, and all things were made through Him.

Colossians 1:15–17 again confirms that Jesus Christ is the first-born over all of creation. And by Him all things were created. This passage also reiterates the eternality of Christ.

The Bible, while not using the term Trinity, plainly teaches that while there is but one true God, He exists as three separate yet equal Persons—and all were present at creation.

Many discussions surround this important doctrine, and can cause division in the church. Remember that the primary truths of the Trinity are presented in God's Word. And be willing to allow that there are secret things that belong to the Lord our God, which have not been revealed (Deuteronomy 29:29).

APOLOGETICS BACKGROUND

How often we hear people speak of God: God is good; God will answer our prayers; God is in control; God has a plan. Yet many of these same people seldom speak the name of Jesus Christ—and may not even believe that salvation comes through Him alone. They deny and fail to understand the important doctrine of the Trinity—three Persons in one God.

These people discount the significance of who Jesus is—that He is 100 percent fully God and 100 percent fully man. Specifically, there are many who claim that Jesus Christ was merely a man—a prophet, the first created being, a sinless and good person—but not God in human flesh. The significance of the doctrine of the Trinity eludes them.

And yet, the New Testament is abundantly clear that Jesus is God. Jesus claimed to be one with the Father (John 10:30–33); He used the title of "I AM" from the Old Testament (John 8:23, 58); He demonstrated His power over nature, disease, demons, and death (Matthew 8); and He forgave sins—something only God can do (Mark 2:1–11).

The Jewish leaders recognized Jesus's claims to deity and tried to stone Him for it (John 5:18, 8:59); ultimately they had Him crucified for blasphemy. Upon seeing the resurrected Christ, Thomas declared, "My Lord and my God!" (John 20:28), and Jesus did not rebuke him but affirmed him for saying so.

Why is it important to believe Trinitarian doctrine and specifically that Jesus is both God and man? Our very salvation requires it. The death of a mere man (no matter how noble) could not provide the purchase price required to redeem other men from their sins against an infinite God. But because Jesus is God, is eternal, and is infinite, He alone is able to satisfy the penalty for those sins by His death.

In addition, Jesus had to be fully human in order to redeem Adam's fallen race. The substitutionary atonement required that Jesus Christ must die as a man to bear judgment for the sins of men. Only the God-man could bridge the gap and bring both God and man together. As a man, He lived a perfect life and is qualified to be our High Priest and Savior (Hebrews 2:17, 7:24–28).

Praise God for His eternal, triune nature, and thank Him that He has provided the way for sinful man to be reconciled with a holy God, through the sacrifice of the perfect God-man, Jesus Christ!

HISTORICAL BACKGROUND

As stated above, the word *Trinity* does not appear in the inspired Word of God. It did not become a formal doctrine of the Church, by name, until the fourth century. This fact has led to numerous debates over the origin of this word and its validity as a doctrine of Scripture.

Many teachers in the history of Christianity have twisted the concept of the Trinity. To misunderstand the nature and character of God is a serious problem. When this misunderstanding leads to a compromise in the true understanding of the gospel, the mistake can rightly be called a heresy—a doctrine that leads to damnation.

A brief look at some of the historical heresies follows. In all cases they deny either the oneness of God, the distinction between the Persons of the Trinity, or the full deity of one or more Persons of the Godhead.

- **Modalism**: This idea suggests that God acts in three different "modes" but is only one Person. God appeared as the "Father" in the Old Testament, as "Jesus" in the earthly ministry, and as the "Spirit" in the present age. Presently, some Pentecostal groups hold to Modalism.

- **Arianism**: Named for the fourth-century teacher Arius, this view teaches that Jesus and the Holy Spirit were created by God the Father. This idea was condemned at the Council of Nicaea in AD 325.

- **Adoptionism**: This view teaches that Jesus was an ordinary man until, at His baptism, He was adopted by the Father and given supernatural powers and the status of "Son of God." Some Unitarians hold this view today.

- **Unitarianism**: This view holds that there is a single God with no distinct Persons. Whether they believe Jesus or the Father is God varies, but many present-day Unitarians reject the pre-existence of Jesus, insisting that He began to exist at the virgin birth.

These various heresies deny the essence of the gospel by corrupting the biblical understanding of atonement, justice, and the effect of Christ's work on the Cross. Church councils were called to deal with mutations of the truth that were being spread in the early church. As a result, the doctrine of the Trinity was codified in the Nicene Creed in 325 and later in the Athanasian Creed. Both of these creeds are the basis of an orthodox understanding of the relationships within the Trinity.

The Trinity is yet another reminder of the immensity of God and our inability to fully understand His awesome nature.

For more information on this topic, see the Online Resource Page.

 **Studying God's Word**

How would you describe the Trinity using an analogy?

Record how each of the following passages informs our understanding of the triune nature of God.

Genesis 1:1–3

Psalm 33:6

John 1:1–5

Isaiah 44:23–24

Colossians 1:15–17

Psalm 104:30

Trinitarian Heresies

Complete the Trinitarian Heresies worksheet.

 ## God's Word in the Real World

1. Why is it important to have a proper understanding of the Trinity?

2. What are some analogies to help us and others understand the Trinity? What are the weaknesses in these analogies?

3. How does understanding the Trinity affect your view of God?

 ## Prayer Requests

The Seven C's of History

11

Key Passages

- Genesis 1:1, 1:31, 3:6–7, 7:11–12, 7:18–21, 11:1–9; Matthew 1:18–23; Colossians 1:19–22; Revelation 21:1–8

What You Will Learn

- The Seven C's of History in order.

- The approximate date in history of each of the Seven C's.

- How the biblical view of history compares to the secular view.

Lesson Overview

The Bible provides a complete history of the universe. The Seven C's of History reveal the major events of history that are foundational to the Bible's important messages.

Memory Verse

Psalm 119:89–90

Forever, O Lord, Your word is settled in heaven. Your faithfulness endures to all generations; You established the earth, and it abides.

🔖 Prepare to Learn

SCRIPTURAL BACKGROUND

Most people look at the Bible as a book that contains interesting stories and theological teaching. They don't understand that the Bible is a history book. Christianity is not based on myths and fables—it is based on real history revealing major events that are foundational to the Bible's important messages. We like to call it the History Book of the Universe!

The accounts are actual historical accounts—Adam was real; he was created on Day Six of creation; his sin cast the whole human race into sin; the Flood was a real, global catastrophic event; Jesus Christ really lived, died, and rose again for the payment of the sins of His people—the Bible is true and can be trusted (1 Corinthians 15:1–4).

When we don't see the Bible as a history book, we are often left unprepared to answer questions accurately and biblically—questions presented to us by our children, family, neighbors, and friends about such things as dinosaurs, fossils, Noah's Ark, Cain's wife, the races, why there is death and suffering, etc. We need to know how to answer these. We need to realize that God's Word cannot be compartmentalized into the "spiritual" area of our lives. It must be integrated into our every waking moment; we

must live, answer questions, and make decisions based on a biblical worldview—based on God's truth, not man's.

The Seven C's of History as presented in this curriculum represent major biblical events that have affected (and will affect) our world history. We start at the beginning—Creation—and follow a timeline of history to its end—Consummation. The Seven C's are:

- **Creation**: In the beginning—about 6,000 years ago—in six 24-hour days, God made a perfect Creation (Genesis 1).

- **Corruption**: The first man, Adam, disobeyed the Creator. His sin brought death and Corruption into God's very good creation (Genesis 2:17).

- **Catastrophe**: Adam's race became so wicked that God judged the world with a great Catastrophe —a global Flood—saving only those on the Ark built by Noah (Genesis 7:23).

- **Confusion**: When Noah's descendants disobeyed God's command to fill the earth, God brought Confusion on their language, forcing them to spread over the earth (Genesis 11:7–8).

- **Christ**: The Creator became a man, Jesus Christ, who obeyed God in everything, unlike the first man, Adam (Matthew 1:21–23).

- **Cross**: Jesus, the Messiah, died on the Cross to pay the penalty for mankind's sin against God. He rose from the dead, providing life for all who trust in Him as Savior (1 Corinthians 15:3–4).

- **Consummation**: One day, at the Consummation, the Creator will remake His creation. He will cast out death and the disobedient, create a new heaven and new earth, and dwell eternally with those who trust in Him (Revelation 21:4).

When we start with the Bible, the history book of the universe, we can develop a worldview that trusts God's Word over man's word—and we will learn to confidently answer the questions we are asked based on the foundation of the truth of God.

APOLOGETICS BACKGROUND

There are basically two views of history— the biblical view, which we outline using the Seven C's of History, and the secular view, which relies on man's ideas from outside the Bible to try and determine the events of the past. These secular ideas are opposed to the Bible's true history. They are prevalent in our culture and often found even in the church today.

Below are some of the erroneous views that stand in opposition to the Seven C's as presented above. It is important to be aware of them and be prepared to give a defense to anyone who questions God's Word (1 Peter 3:15).

- **Creation**: The universe was created from a big bang about 13 billion years ago; the earth formed about 4.5 billion years ago. Animals and man have evolved to their present state.

- **Corruption**: The world has always had disease, struggle, and death. Sin and guilt are just psychological conditions that must be overcome.

- **Catastrophe**: If there was a flood, it was a local flood that only affected the Mesopotamian region.

- **Confusion**: There are different races of mankind, and these races reflect different levels of evolutionary development.

- **Christ**: If Jesus even lived, then He was a good man or a prophet, or perhaps even our "Savior," but He is not the Creator.

- **Cross**: Jesus's death on the Cross shows that He identified with us in our suffering, but in and of itself it has no significance for salvation.

- **Consummation**: Either all men will be saved because God is loving and would never send anyone to hell, or there is no afterlife, but people return to the dust when they die.

The Word of God can be trusted, not only when it speaks of spiritual and moral principles, but also when it speaks on history and science. As Jesus told Nicodemus, "If I have told you earthly things and you do not believe, how will you believe if I tell you heavenly things?" (John 3:12). In other words, if we can't believe the Bible's history, starting in Genesis, why should we believe its gospel message? If we can't trust the Bible's history in the first several chapters, then when can we start trusting it?

HISTORICAL BACKGROUND

Those who hold to an old-earth, evolutionary view of history have a completely different worldview from those who hold to the biblical creation view—the Seven C's of History. The first is a naturalistic (no God) view that promotes autonomous human reason, ignoring God's written revelation. The other is a "supernaturalistic" view, recognizing God's involvement in the affairs of man, which starts from God's perfect revelation—the Bible. These two views are diametrically opposed to one another.

One of the main issues separating these two views concerns the age of the earth. Before the 1700s, it was the general consensus of the church that God created the world, as described in the book of Genesis, around 4,000 to 6,000 years ago. Since then, because of scientific and geological "evidences" of a much older world, many Christians have felt the need to accommodate these erroneous ideas—and have compromised God's Word by manipulating it to say things it does not say.

The chart below indicates some past scholars and historians who believed that the earth was young. They calculated the age of the earth based on their study and trust in God's Word.

Chronologist	When Lived	Calculated Date of Creation (BC)
Julius Africanus	c. 250	5501
George Syncellus	c. 800	5492
John Jackson	c. 1750	5426
William Hales	c. 1850	5411
Eusebius	c. 350	5199
Marianus Scotus	c. 1050	4192
Thomas Lydiat	c. 1600	4103
M. Michael Maestlinus	c. 1600	4079
Jacob Salianus	c. 1600	4053
H. Spondanus	c. 1600	4051
J. Cappellus	c. 1600	4005
J. Ussher	c. 1650	4004
E. Greswell	c. 1830	4004
D. Petavius	c. 1630	3983
C. Longomontanus	c. 1600	3966
P. Melanchthon	c. 1550	3964
A. Salmeron	c. 1600	3958
J. Scaliger	c. 1600	3949
M. Beroaldus	c. 1550	3927
A. Helwigius	c. 1650	3836

Note: c means circa = approximately

Again, keep in mind that the old-earth theory did not become the scientific consensus until the late 1700s. This is when the study of geology became popular and geologists began to date the rock layers as millions of years old. Unfortunately, many theologians and church leaders have accepted these new ideas, rejected the clear teachings of Scripture about a young earth, and pursued old-earth tenets that undermine the Bible's gospel message.

Our resolve to stand firm on God's Word must be strong in this area as we determine to contend for the faith as recorded in Scripture (Jude 1:3).

For more information on this topic, see the Online Resource Page.

Studying God's Word

Place the following in chronological order without using any references: Moses, Abraham, Battle of Jericho, Christ's birth, Tower of Babel, Adam, the Flood.

 ## Comparing the Views

Record details of each of the Seven C's of History in the class handout as the lesson progresses.

 ## God's Word in the Real World

1. How do you see this framework for history being helpful as you interact with others?

2. Which of these seven events does the church challenge the most? Why?

 ## Prayer Requests

12
What Is the Gospel?

Key Passages

- Genesis 1:31–2:4, 3:6–7, 3:21–23, 6:5–8, 8:1, 8:15–17, 11:1–9; Romans 3:19–26, 5:12, 5:18–19; John 1:14–17; 1 Corinthians 15:1–5; 2 Corinthians 5:21; Revelation 21:1–8

What You Will Learn

- What the central theme of the Bible is.

- How to relate the gospel through the Seven C's of History framework.

- Why the good news only makes sense in light of the bad news.

Lesson Overview

The Seven C's of History offer a framework for sharing the gospel by starting with the bad news of sin and moving to the good news of Christ's redemption.

Memory Verse

Psalm 119:89–90
Forever, O Lord, Your word is settled in heaven. Your faithfulness endures to all generations; You established the earth, and it abides.

📖 Prepare to Learn

SCRIPTURAL BACKGROUND

In past lessons we have been introduced to the Bible—where it came from, how to study it, why we can believe it. These are all critical areas of learning for all of us, but what is the central message of the Bible? Let's start at the beginning. What happened long ago in the Garden of Eden—Adam's Fall into sin—has affected us all.

God's first proclamation of a coming Redeemer who would crush the serpent's head appeared in Genesis (Genesis 3:15). The death and Resurrection of Jesus the Messiah fulfilled this prophecy—revealing God's plan of redemption.

To truly understand the good news of the Bible, we must grasp the bad news of the Bible first. Because God is a holy God—righteous and separate from sin—He cannot dwell with sinful man, and His perfect justice demands that He punish disobedience. The Bible tells us that all have sinned and come short of the glory of God (Romans 3:23) and that the wages of sin is death (Romans 6:23). This is the bad news—that all people are separated from God, born spiritually dead (Ephesians 2:1), under His just penalty, and destined for an eternity in hell.

There is absolutely no way that we can work our way to God or ever be good enough to merit eternal life. In fact, the Bible makes it clear that there are no good works that will commend us to God.

> Isaiah 64:6—But we are all like an unclean thing, and all our righteousnesses are like filthy rags; we all fade as a leaf, and our iniquities, like the wind, have taken us away.

> Ephesians 2:8–9—For by grace you have been saved through faith, and that not of yourselves; it is the gift of God, not of works, lest anyone should boast.

> Titus 3:5—Not by works of righteousness which we have done, but according to His mercy He saved us . . . .

God sent His own Son, Jesus, to become a man, live a sinless life, and then die on the Cross, paying the penalty of death that we all deserve. "God made Him who knew no sin to be sin for us, that we might become the righteousness of God in Him" (2 Corinthians 5:21). In the death of Christ, we see the justice of God satisfied and the love of God demonstrated (Romans 5:8).

So, what do we need to do to receive forgiveness for our sins against God and inherit eternal life? The Apostle Paul makes the essential elements of the gospel clear.

Moreover, brethren, I declare to you the gospel which I preached to you . . . . For I delivered to you first of all that which I also received: that Christ died for our sins according to the Scriptures, and that He was buried, and that He rose again the third day according to the Scriptures (1 Corinthians 15:1–4).

Jesus's death for our sins, His burial, and His Resurrection are the heart of the good news. And how must we respond to spend eternity with our Creator?

Mark 1:14–15—Jesus came to Galilee, preaching the gospel of the kingdom of God, and saying, "The time is fulfilled, and the kingdom of God is at hand. Repent, and believe in the gospel."

John 3:16—For God so loved the world that He gave His only begotten Son, that whoever believes in Him should not perish but have everlasting life.

Acts 16:30–31—And he brought them out and said, "Sirs, what must I do to be saved?" So they said, "Believe on the Lord Jesus Christ, and you will be saved."

Acts 20:20–21—I kept back nothing that was helpful, but proclaimed it to you, and taught you publicly and from house to house, testifying to Jews, and also to Greeks, repentance toward God and faith toward our Lord Jesus Christ.

Romans 10:9–10—That if you confess with your mouth the Lord Jesus and believe in your heart that God has raised Him from the dead, you will be saved.

Repentance of one's sin, and trust in Christ as Savior and Lord are all that is required to be saved. And when that occurs in our hearts, we are adopted by God as His children, joint heirs with Christ (Ephesians 1:5; Romans 8:16–17); we are born again to a new and living hope (1 Peter 1:3); we become new creations in Christ (2 Corinthians 5:17); and we have the sure hope of eternal life (Titus 1:2). It is not until we grasp the bad news— we are sinners in desperate need of a Savior—that we will appreciate the good news—we can be reconciled to God by the perfect sacrifice of Jesus Christ. Praise be to God for His grace and mercy demonstrated in the good news of the gospel—the central theme of the Bible!

APOLOGETICS BACKGROUND

In today's pluralistic society with its many religions and insistence on tolerance for all views, it is important that we understand that the good news of the Bible is not just one way among many.

Rather, Jesus and the apostles make it abundantly clear that faith in this gospel message is the ONLY way to be reconciled to God. Jesus is the ONLY mediator between man and God (1 Timothy 2:5).

> Jesus said to him, "I am the way, the truth, and the life. No one comes to the Father except through Me" (John 14:6).

> Nor is there salvation in any other, for there is no other name [Jesus] under heaven given among men by which we must be saved (Acts 4:12).

Why is Jesus the only way? Because, as theologian Dr. Bruce Ware puts it:

- Christ alone was conceived by the Holy Spirit and born of a virgin and as such, He alone qualifies to be Savior (Isaiah 7:14; Matthew 1:18–25; Luke 1:26–38).

- Christ alone is God incarnate and as such, He alone qualifies to be Savior (John 1:1–18; Hebrews 1:1–3, 2:14–18; Philippians 2:5–11; 1 Timothy 2:5–6).

- Christ alone lived a sinless life and as such, He alone qualifies to be Savior (2 Corinthians 5:21; Hebrews 4:15, 7:23–28, 9:13–14; 1 Peter 2:21–24).

- Christ alone died a penal, substitutionary death and as such, He alone qualifies to be Savior (Isaiah 53:4–6; Romans 3:21–26; 2 Corinthians 5:21).

- Christ alone rose from the dead, triumphant over sin and as such, He alone qualifies to be Savior (Acts 2:22–24; Romans 4:25; 1 Corinthians 15:3–8).[1]

No other person, and no man-made religion, offers the true path of salvation and reconciliation with God. Merely acknowledging that God exists, or believing there is a God, does not save anyone. Scripture tells us that even the demons believe (James 2:19). It is only through repentance and faith in Jesus and His work on the Cross that anyone can be saved.

HISTORICAL BACKGROUND

The early church preached the true gospel amidst much opposition. For the first two centuries, Christians were persecuted, killed, ostracized, and considered second-class citizens. Yet, the gospel spread and the blood of the martyrs only seemed to validate the message, increasing its power.

It was in AD 312 that the Roman Emperor Constantine was converted to Christianity and, as a result, he commanded official toleration of Christianity, and other religions. And then, in 380, Emperor Theodosius made

---

1 Bruce Ware, "Only One Way? The Exclusivity of Jesus Christ and the Gospel," http://www.christianity.com/christian%20foundations/christianity%20main/11602124.

Christianity the official religion of the empire. From this point on, Christians could worship openly, and they enjoyed the protection and favor of the government.

Throughout the following centuries, segments of the church began to include doctrines and practices that were not found in the Bible nor were part of the early church's beliefs and traditions. These included the special authority of the Pope, the concept of purgatory as a place for after-life purification of sins, the immaculate conception and assumption of Mary, the doctrine of transubstantiation (that the bread in the Eucharist becomes the true body of Christ and the wine becomes His blood), and the general belief that one's good works had to outweigh the bad in order to attain eternal life.

While the true gospel had been corrupted by officials in the church, God always preserved a remnant who believed the truth of His Word. And in the fifteenth and sixteenth centuries, this remnant courageously began the movement known as the Reformation. God used these believers to restore the gospel of justification by faith in Christ alone, by grace alone—through the truth of the Bible alone.

Today, we again find the professing church corrupted and moving away from the truth and simplicity of the gospel message according to God's Word. Many churches are distorting the Word of God in hopes of attracting more people to their services. These false messages can range from prosperity preaching (that God wants us all to be healthy and wealthy), to easy believism (just say a few words and you will be saved for eternity), to counseling sessions based on secular psychology (come see us and we can fix your life right up), to universalism (anyone can get to heaven as long as you are sincere in what you believe), and the list goes on—as far as man's corrupted mind will take it.

The message of the gospel is clear. We are saved through repentance and faith in the God-Man, Jesus Christ, who came to earth, died for the sins of His people, and rose again from the dead (1 Corinthians 15:3–4). He is the only Mediator and He sits at the right hand of God the Father, waiting to make His enemies His footstool (Hebrews 10:13).

For more information on this topic, see the Online Resource Page.

 Studying God's Word

Which should come first, good news or bad news? Why?

_____

_____

_____

_____

Take notes as you study the following passages.

1 Corinthians 15:1–5

_____

_____

_____

The Gospel Through the Seven C's of History

Take notes on your class worksheet as you work through each of
the Seven C's and how they relate to the gospel.

God's Word in the Real World

1. Do you see this method of presenting the gospel being
   useful? Why?

2. Why is it essential to understand the historical relationship between the first Adam and the Last Adam?

3. Is it important to understand where sin came from in order to understand the gospel rightly?

4. What do you see as the biggest stumbling blocks for unbelievers as you share the truth of God's Word with them?

5. What areas do you need to grow in to be able to understand and share the gospel with others?

Prayer Requests

Value of a Biblical Worldview

Key Passage

- Colossians 2:1–10; Proverbs 4:1–9; 1 Timothy 6:20–21

What You Will Learn

- The areas in the culture where the Bible is set aside as the absolute authority.

- How your personal views of the world may or may not be out of line with biblical truths.

Lesson Overview

God has graciously given us His Word, and we should strive to conform every thought that we have to the truth revealed in Scripture.

Memory Verse

Psalm 119:89–90
Forever, O Lord, Your word is settled in heaven. Your faithfulness endures to all generations; You established the earth, and it abides.

📖 Prepare to Learn

SCRIPTURAL BACKGROUND

For the past 12 lessons, we have been looking at many different ideas concerning the truthfulness and usefulness of God's Word. This lesson is intended to be a wrap-up for the quarter and to bring back into focus the importance of God's Word as the foundation for our lives. We have looked at how to study the Bible, how we got the Bible, how important it is to defend the Bible, the nature of God, and a framework for understanding biblical history. All of these things set the stage for a chronological study through the Bible.

Scripture makes it abundantly clear that the words of God are the source of wisdom, knowledge, understanding, and truth. Wisdom begins with a fear of the Lord (Job 28:28; Psalm 111:10; Proverbs 1:7, 9:10, 15:33). If we are to base our lives on any source or system other than the Bible, we are acting as fools.

Apart from the truths in the Bible, we can know little about the true nature of the world around us. Whether we are trying to understand the origin of the world, why bad things happen, or the nature of humanity, we must start with the Bible to get a correct picture. All of these issues are tied to the doctrines we find in Scripture. Doctrine is important, and it must be rightly taught. In order to understand what ideas are true,

we must compare them to Scripture—we must see through biblical glasses.

This is the admonition Paul gave to young Timothy when he wrote to him in 1 Timothy 6:20–21. People have strayed from the faith by following ideas that were not founded in God's truth. Timothy was to protect his flock from these false teachings and hold to the clear teachings he had received. Wisdom based in man's reasoning and apart from God is false knowledge.

Paul expanded upon this concept in Colossians 2:1–10. In this passage, the wisdom of God is linked directly to the person of Christ. It is in Christ, not in the philosophies or traditions of men, that we find all the treasures of wisdom and knowledge. Thinking that starts from man's reasoning alone is deceitful and will lead to error. We received the truths of Christ in faith, and we should continue to walk with Him in faith. If we do anything other than that, we have cheated ourselves and missed the richness of Christ and the mystery of His coming to this earth to save us from our sins.

APOLOGETICS BACKGROUND

Some would look at Colossians 2 and suggest that it is wrong for Christians to study philosophy. However, a more careful examination of the passage only warns against philosophies and traditions that are not centered on Christ. We should long for knowledge that is in Christ and seek diligently to understand the world He has created in light of that truth. We need to make sure that we are looking at the world with biblical glasses.

We can only have unity in truth. Those who reject the clear teachings of Scripture and add tradition or worldly wisdom to their theology should be identified and avoided (Romans 16:17–18). There is a myth in our pluralistic society that says we can accept every view as a valid view. This is the worldly philosophy of relativism, and it stands in direct opposition to the biblical view of absolute truth. We must unashamedly proclaim that the gospel of Jesus Christ as revealed in the Bible is the only hope for mankind (Romans 1:15–17).

As we disciple new believers and proclaim truth to the world around us, we must make it clear that the knowledge we seek is found in God. There are those who continually seek after knowledge but never come to an understanding of the truth because they ignore that all of these things are found in Christ (2 Timothy 3:6–7). As followers of Christ, we should pray that His Spirit will enable us to grasp the truth He has revealed to us in His Word.

HISTORICAL BACKGROUND

Throughout church history there have been those who have rejected the authority of the Bible and tried to impose their personal philosophies on God. The letter to the Colossians was likely aimed, in part, at discrediting philosophies that were blending Jewish traditions or mystical practices with the truths of Christ. Paul warned them strongly against philosophies that were not simply founded upon Christ.

Throughout history, people have tried mixing their own ideas with the worship of God. As we read the Old Testament accounts, people were constantly adding idolatrous practices to the pure worship that God desired. This tendency is no different in the hearts of people two thousand years ago than it is today. People always try to add their own works and ideas to what God has revealed to them.

Various church councils and reformations happened in response to these attacks on the truths of Scripture. Understanding these attacks can help us to understand the attacks on the gospel today. History repeats itself, and we can see reflections of past errors in the movements on the fringes of the church today. Understanding how believers in Christ have dealt with these issues—using Scripture—can help us face these challenges today. We look to God's Word as the authority.

For more information on this topic, see the Online Resource Page.

Studying God's Word

How do each of the passages below relate to our worldview? Where should we go to find wisdom and truth?

Colossians 2:1–10

Proverbs 4:1–9

1 Timothy 6:20–21

God's Word in the Real World

1. In what areas in our culture do we see a lack of applying biblical truths?

2. In what areas in the church do we see a lack of applying biblical truths?

3. Are there areas in your school studies where you see a contradiction between what is being taught and what the Bible teaches?

4. How do most people in our society view the idea that Jesus Christ provides the only way of salvation and access to heaven?

5. Are there areas that you can identify where your thoughts and beliefs are not lining up with what Scripture teaches?

Prayer Requests